AF382900

HOW TO WRITE A SUCCESSFUL CV

Win over any recruiter with a perfectly crafted CV

Written by Pierre Latour
Translated by Emma Hanna

Coaching 50MINUTES.com

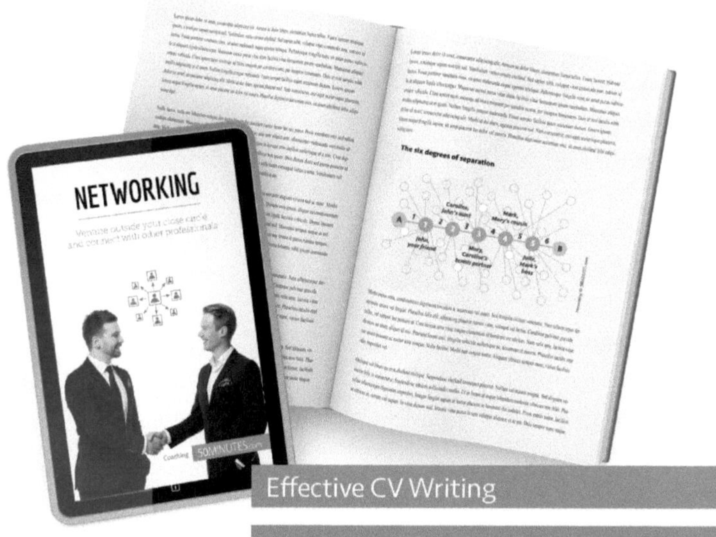

HOW TO WRITE A SUCCESSFUL CV

- **Problem:** how can I improve my CV?
- **Uses:** a jobseeker's CV is their most effective means of showcasing their skills and experience during their search. It is the key to convincing a potential future employer that they should be advanced to the next stage of the recruitment process.
- **Professional context:** job search.
- **FAQs:**
  - Should I include a photo with my CV?
  - Should I accompany my CV with a cover letter?
  - How should I structure my CV?
  - What about the European CV format?
  - How should I organise the information?
  - What style should I use?
  - How long should my CV be?
  - How should I structure my professional experiences?
  - How can I justify being fired or holding posts

for a short period of time?

  ◦ Should I mention the salary I am hoping to receive in my CV?

Whether you have just finished your studies or you are between jobs, your *curriculum vitae* – a Latin phrase which can be translated as "the course of [your] life" – should now be your greatest ally in the professional world. In addition to giving anyone who reads it a clear idea of your training and experience, your CV should demonstrate your capabilities and reflect your ability to put your ideas and ambitions into words.

This means that neglecting your CV is a fatal mistake which should be avoided at all costs. However, if you take control of the situation, you will be ready to show your future employer that they need you and that you are the most suitable candidate for the job you are applying for.

JOB HUNTING: THE BASICS

In the world of work, your CV will act as your letter of introduction to any employer who does not know you. No matter how inconsequential your CV may seem, it plays a crucial role when you apply for a job: it is the first thing a recruiter will look at, and it plays the role of your initial sales pitch. At this stage, it is imperative to use every weapon at your disposal in order to make a good impression.

Your CV will have to adhere to certain standards regarding the quality of both its form and its content in order to capture a recruiter's full attention. If you respect these conventions, your potential employer is more likely to give your application the consideration it deserves and notice more of the details in your profile.

CONVINCE THEM!

Submitting a CV, whether by post or online, is the first step in the recruitment and selection process. The goal is to present your profile to your employer in an effective manner, highlighting your strengths and your future prospects in order to make them take an interest in you. Always keep in mind that you need to convince the recruiter that you fit the required profile for the position on offer! Given how little time the recruiter will devote to reading your CV, there can be no doubt that writing it is no trivial matter.

It is all a question of making your CV stand out from those sent in by other candidates (of whom there will doubtless be many). This is no small feat, given that you will not only have to make it clear that you have the skills and knowledge that the position requires, but also that your profile has an edge over those of the other candidates. This can be particularly tricky to achieve when applying for posts without a recommendation from another employee or an acquaintance to boost your chances.

A CV IS NOT A SUBSTITUTE FOR AN INTERVIEW

While writing your CV, do not forget that you could be called in for an interview. In this situation, your CV will remain your greatest ally, as it will give the recruiter an overview of your profile and your professional and academic path thus far at a glance, provided it is well written and structured. The impression the recruiter is left with upon reading your CV will indirectly colour the way they view your application as a whole.

You should also bear in mind that a recruiter may bring up any of the details you include in your CV, in which case you will have to explain their relevance to the position you are applying for. As such, padding out or falsifying your CV is inadvisable, as a trick question during the interview could easily catch you out and ruin your chances of getting the job. It is better to highlight your genuine skills and strengths.

MAKE SURE YOUR CV FITS THE BILL

The purpose of a CV is to convince the recruiter of your worth at a glance, meaning that you must give an effective overview of your education, professional history and personal life (where relevant). This will allow any potential employer to understand the specific strengths and qualities that make your profile unique. If the recruiter reaches this point and decides to read your CV more closely, it is vital that you make this task easier for them by structuring all the information clearly. Every detail should indicate further added value.

To maximise your chances of being called in for an interview and progressing through the recruitment process, your CV should be adapted to the post that you are applying for; in other words, you should make sure to emphasise the skills which are in line with the job on offer. At this stage, it is crucial to get a clear idea of the company that you are applying to – for example, via their website – so that you can understand their vision and values and therefore structure your own arguments in a way that resonates with them.

Once you have completed your analysis of the company, move on to drawing up a list of all the defining characteristics of your professional trajectory thus far, ranging from the most trivial to the most meaningful experiences, then use the position you are applying for to help you select the most relevant parts of that list to include when writing your CV. This approach means that it is worthwhile to start writing a new CV from scratch and to review each stage of your trajectory so that you have a better idea of which experiences and elements to highlight based on the job in question.

This approach has multiple advantages:

- you gain familiarity with the content of your CV;
- you gain experience in the process of writing a CV.

THE ESSENTIALS

Naturally, your CV should include a full list of your contact details, allowing a potential employer to get in touch with you quickly and easily, whether to arrange a face-to-face interview or for a telephone interview. It is particularly important to include:

- your full name;
- your date of birth;
- your address;
- your email address (use a professional-sounding address, e.g. name.surname@xxx.com);
- your telephone number (mobile or landline).

EXTRA INFORMATION

Add a personal statement that sums up your profile in a few words. Avoid phrases like "Enthusiastic young graduate seeking a fulfilling position" which are insubstantial and do not provide any information about your abilities; instead, take the opportunity to emphasise your skills and experience with a statement such as "Financial manager with strong organisational skills and five years of experience in the pharmaceutical sector".

It is also worth including these basic but essential details on the other documents submitted with your application, as recruiters may print out your CV to discuss it with a colleague and then have difficulty finding your application again afterwards – do not make it any harder for them!

DIVIDE YOUR CV INTO THREE MAIN SECTIONS

A conventional CV should be divided into three separate, easily identifiable sections:

- education;
- professional experience;
- interests and activities.

For each section, you must select the things that are most relevant to the job you are applying for to include in your CV. Review each stage of your professional, academic and extra-curricular paths and identify any experiences or skills which will help you stand out. This standard structure will help the recruiter to identify your knowledge, skills, experience and areas of expertise, as well as some indications about your personality. Generally speaking, you should choose the information you include in your CV based on the job you are applying for.

REVERSE CHRONOLOGICAL ORDER

The information included in a CV is conventionally structured in reverse chronological order, meaning that your most recent training and experiences should be mentioned first.

This is standard practice because it has the advantage of drawing attention to your most recent experience, which tends to be the most relevant. Naturally, recruiters prefer this way of structuring information because they will be most interested in your

Section one: professional experience

Highlight each post you have held that has provided you with skills and experience which are relevant to the job you are applying for. You can also list your responsibilities and greatest achievements alongside the most important jobs you have held, whereas you can limit the extra information you include about less relevant jobs, or jobs which you held a long time ago, to the length of time you worked there. These descriptions should be written in the form of a bullet-point list in order to show off your knowledge and expertise effectively. You should also include the start and end dates of each job, preferably the month and year.

EXTRA INFORMATION

Do not underestimate the impact that periods of inactivity can have on your CV. Given that they form an important part of your life, and that lying about them could cause problems for you, think about how you could justify them during an interview.

- **Extra advice for experienced employees:** stick to the essentials; there is no point in listing every position you have held since you finished your education. Employers will only really take your experiences and jobs from the past five to ten years into account.
- **Extra advice for recent graduates:**
  - the "Education" section should come before the "Professional experience" section, given that it will cover the most important points of your application;
  - naturally, you should emphasise any internships or student jobs that you have had in order to show that you have experience (no matter how fleeting) with the job market;
  - if you do not have any relevant experience, try to compensate by making a note of any practical experience you gained during your studies (group work, projects, etc.).

Section two: education

List any training you have undertaken in reverse chronological order. However, you should also be precise and focus on the essentials – in other words, only make a note of any specialisations if they correspond to an aspect of the position you are applying for.

- **It can be useful** to go into more detail about the academic experiences which are most relevant to the position. As such, you should consider providing more information about any projects you completed or extra courses you took, as these will catch the recruiter's attention as they read your CV.
- **It is pointless** to list every single course you have ever taken. Ideally you should only include the main education you have received (at training centres, universities, business schools, etc.), as well as your high school if it has a good reputation. Recruiters do not want to know everything – they just want the broad strokes.

If you did not finish a course or if you failed the final exam, you should still include it in your CV and simply note that your training was "incomplete". In the recruiter's mind, there may be a good reason for an unfinished degree which could be explained during an interview, and mentioning this training is proof of an additional positive experience from which you probably gained at least some skills and knowledge.

Section three: interests and activities

Avoid letting this section of your CV get cluttered. The goal here should be to use your extra-curricular activities to make yourself stand out even more, so try to stick to mentioning skills related to the job, such as knowledge of foreign languages or IT skills.

Do not forget to specify your level of expertise regarding these two points, and keep your vocabulary consistent throughout the CV: for example, "expert", "capable", and "beginner", plus "native language", "fluent", and "conversational". You should also expect to be tested on these skills during an interview. Once again, you should avoid including false information, as this could spell disaster during an interview. In any case, your level of expertise should always be at least equal to the level required by the company.

Finally, finish this section by listing your hobbies and pastimes, bearing in mind that your aim should be to stick to the essentials and to make yourself stand out. Try to avoid mentioning anything that does not imply underlying skills or abilities which align with the position on offer and with your professional ambitions.

This section of your CV will also give your employer some indication of your personality, as it may hint at team spirit, social engagement, curiosity, and so on. It can often be a way of creating a connection with the recruiter if you share a common passion. On the other hand, avoid mentioning any activity that hints at your political, religious or philosophical beliefs, as this could work against you.

TOP TIPS

- Avoid using coloured paper and opt instead for a plain, clear, well-structured CV. If you do use colours in your CV, use them consistently and sparingly (for example, only for the section headings).
- Start your CV with a short, snappy personal statement, which should cover the defining characteristics of your profile.
- Opt for traditional, serious fonts such as Arial, Times New Roman or Calibri, instead of more outlandish fonts (exceptions can be made if you are applying for a creative post).
- Use bold over italics where possible. Bold can be used to draw the recruiter's attention, to give the text structure, and to highlight the most important information, whereas italics are generally more difficult to read.
- Adapt the vocabulary you use and the skills you emphasise based on what the employer is looking for – show them that you are the ideal candidate.
- When listing information, use bullet points or

hyphenated lists to organise the information instead of presenting it in long, convoluted paragraphs. This will make the CV easier to read and create a more positive impression.

- Use a consistent style throughout your CV. For example, if you mention the name of the last company you worked for, followed by the position you held there, use this same order when listing your previous jobs. You should also follow this principle when describing your academic history.

- Be careful with your spelling and grammar. Ask an acquaintance with a gift for writing to proofread your CV before you submit it. Recruiters often pay special attention to these sorts of things and will not waste their time on a CV which is chock-full of mistakes.

- Ask your friends for their advice – have them read over your CV to get their opinion. This is a simple step which lets you check that the document is coherent and accurately reflects your profile.

- Keep your CV up to date. Make sure that your contact details (telephone number, address, email address), experience and skills acquired through your most recent jobs, voluntary work and training are all accurate, as you should be ready to produce your CV at any time.

FAQS

SHOULD I INCLUDE A PHOTO WITH MY CV?

Although it is not compulsory, some people recommend including a photo of yourself in the upper right corner of your CV. If you decide to attach a photo, make sure that it is appropriate and professional – never use a photo from a holiday, a party or a trip to the beach. Generally speaking, you should not include a photo unless you have one that shows you at your best in a professional setting.

PERSONAL VS. PRIVATE LIFE

While looking for a job, consider updating your social network profiles to ensure that a recruiter who is looking for information about you on sites such as Facebook, LinkedIn or Viadeo will only be able to find limited information which is of a professional nature. If your private life is too visible it can hurt your chances.

SHOULD I ACCOMPANY MY CV WITH A COVER LETTER?

Cover letters are indispensable. In fact, they play the key role of complementing your CV, because they are planned and written with the specific company and position you are applying for in mind. The purpose of a cover letter is to help your potential employer to draw connections between your profile, personality, skills (as mentioned in your CV) and motivation. Try to put yourself in the recruiter's shoes and sell yourself based on your strengths, always asking yourself: "what is the most effective way of persuading them that I am a good fit for their company?"

If you are sending a spontaneous application, do not hesitate to send your CV and cover letter to your contacts and acquaintances who work in the company and ask them to recommend you to the human resources department or to their colleagues, as this will improve your chances.

HOW SHOULD I STRUCTURE MY CV?

Most recruiters prefer CVs which are divided into three sections, as this allows them to quickly gauge the candidate's profile. The following structure is standard:

- Professional experience
- Education
- Interests and activities

However, creativity may be appreciated by recruiters if you are applying for a more creatively-oriented position, particularly in the fields of art and culture. For those who have just graduated and who have little to no professional experience, the position of the "Professional experience" and "Education" sections should usually be reversed.

WHAT ABOUT THE EUROPEAN CV FORMAT?

Unless it has been requested by the recruiter, you should generally avoid the European CV format (also known as the Europass format) for two main reasons:

- it can often come across as long and disorganised because it includes more pages but not a lot of additional information;
- it is not very easy to read, which is particularly frowned upon given how little time recruiters take to look through a CV.

HOW SHOULD I ORGANISE THE INFORMATION?

All the information and the stages of your professional trajectory should be listed in reverse chronological order, from most to least recent.

WHAT STYLE SHOULD I USE?

Avoid long paragraphs and sentences, and use bullet points where possible, though no more than two or three. Remember that the aim is to stick to the essential.

HOW LONG SHOULD MY CV BE?

It is advisable to keep your CV short, in order to make it easier to read. In general, it should be either one or two A4 pages in length, depending on the country, sector and company you are applying to – for example, in the UK, a length of two A4 pages is fairly standard, whereas one-page "résumés" are the norm in the USA. Similarly, investment banks tend to prefer one-page CVs which can be easily perused, but in the academic sector, researchers often list all of the conferences they have spoken at and papers they have published.

If you are having trouble getting your CV to fit onto one or two pages, you are probably including unnecessary experiences or training. Do not be tempted to cheat by reducing the font to less than 11 pts or reducing the margins, as this will not improve your chances – quite the opposite!

HOW SHOULD I STRUCTURE MY PROFESSIONAL EXPERIENCES?

Recruiters will above all be looking for a sense of narrative that gives your CV meaning, so to present yourself in the best light possible, try to make the links between your training and the previous positions you have held as clear as possible.

HOW CAN I JUSTIFY BEING FIRED OR HOLDING POSTS FOR A SHORT PERIOD OF TIME?

Generally speaking, recruiters prefer candidates whom they can expect to be stable, meaning those who have had several significant professional experiences lasting a year and a half or more. If you have had jobs for a shorter period of time because you were hired on a fixed-term contract, you should always specify this.

- If you have been fired, you must be prepared to explain the situation to the recruiter during an interview.
- If you were dismissed for economic reasons, this is sufficient explanation.

When discussing sensitive topics with a recruiter, it is important not to criticise your old company. It is better to demonstrate that you have learned from these experiences, even if the wound still stings.

SHOULD I MENTION THE SALARY I AM HOPING TO RECEIVE IN MY CV?

Never mention the salary you are hoping to receive in your CV. However, you should look into the salary bracket that corresponds to the position you are aiming for while preparing for your interview, particularly by:

- looking at studies available online and/or in specialised magazines;
- asking any friends who work in that sector;
- talking to headhunting consultancies.

EXAMPLE CV

Thomas HAMILTON
3 Flint Street, London, UK
17/05/1990
077xxxxxxx
thomas.hamilton@gmail.com

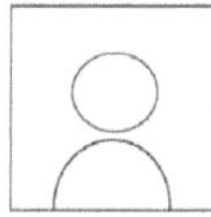

Seasoned negotiator with four years' experience in the legal sector and a talent for finding creative solutions.

Professional Experience

12/2013 – present
Assistant to the Fiscal Crime Liaison Officer, French Embassy, London, UK
- Maintaining effective liaison between HMRC and the relevant French/Foreign and Commonwealth Office departments.
- Negotiating opportunities for cooperation with French Authorities in the field of fiscal fraud investigation.

10/2013 – 12/2013
Sales assistant (fixed term contract), Selfridges, London, UK
Prospecting for new clients and advising them on purchase options.

01/2012 – 07/2012
Store manager, Decathlon sports shop, Oxford, UK
Advising clients, managing stock supplies and inventories.

Education

09/2011 – 06/2013
MSc Management, University of Grenoble, France
- University of Grenoble, France (1st year)
- University of British Colombia, Canada (1st term of 2nd year)
- University of Vienna, Austria (2nd term of 2nd year)

09/2007 – 06/2011
BSc Business Economics, London School of Economics, UK

Extracurricular Activities

2011 – 2012
Council member, Students' Union, London School of Economics
Organising events, managing Students' Union finances

2008 – 2010
Scout leader, Oxford, UK
Organising summer camps to entertain groups of boys aged 8-12

Languages

- English: native
- French: proficient
- German: conversational

We want to hear from you!
Leave a comment on your online library
and share your favourite books on social media!

50MINUTES.com
History
Business
Coaching
Book Review
Health & Wellbeing
ISHIKAWA DIAGRAM
Anticipate and solve problems within your business
Material Method Machine
Mother Nature Measure Men
THE BATTLE OF AUSTERLITZ
NETWORKING
IMPROVE YOUR GENERAL KNOWLEDGE
IN A BLINK OF AN EYE !
www.50minutes.com

www.50minutes.com

Ebook EAN: 9782806269775

Paperback EAN: 9782808006118

Legal Deposit: D/2017/12603/846

Cover: © Primento

Digital conception by Primento, the digital partner of publishers.